CLARITY IS POWER

"Clarity is Power" book series, is a collection of wisdom from thought-provoking Q and A with renowned Mahatria. His unique gift of answering questions spontaneously is captured in this book, offering life-changing insights.

The "Clarity is Power" series comprises 11 illuminating volumes, each addressing essential aspects of life:

1. Attitudes
2. Self-Discipline
3. Emotional Development
4. Relationships
5. Marriage
6. Parenting
7. Student Life
8. Career Growth
9. Leadership and Entrepreneurship
10. Spirituality
11. Faith

Mahatria Spiritualist | Thought leader | Diviner of infinitheism

For nearly three decades, Mahatria has empowered millions worldwide to achieve holistic abundance. His profound wisdom uplifts people in health, wealth, love, bliss, and spirituality.

infinitheism, the path divined by Mahatria, inspires breakthroughs for anyone who ardently desires abundance by transforming the human spirit to have faith in its infinite potential.

First published in India

Manjul Publishing House

• 2nd Floor, Usha Preet Complex,
42 Malviya Nagar, Bhopal 462 003 - India
• C-16, Sector 3, Noida, Uttar Pradesh 201301 – India
Website: www.manjulindia.com

Distribution Centres:
Ahmedabad, Bengaluru, Bhopal, Kolkata, Chennai,
Hyderabad, Mumbai, New Delhi, Pune

In association with:

infinitheism

3, 3rd Cross Road, R A Puram,
Chennai, Tamil Nadu, India
www.infinitheism.com

LEADERSHIP and ENTREPRENEURSHIP
(CLARITY IS POWER)

by

This edition first published in 2016
Third impression 2024

ISBN 978-93-5543-882-9

Printed and bound in India by Thomson Press (India) Ltd.

LEADERSHIP AND ENTREPRENEURSHIP

mahātria

CONTENTS

1	I am a self-made man and a first-generation entrepreneur. Though I am doing reasonably well in my business, of late, I am feeling a bit stagnated. Too many issues are demanding my personal focus. How do I take my business from here? Please help.	6
2	How to develop a peaceful and happy environment at workplace?	12
3	With such high attrition rates how do we build a stable organisation?	18
4	I am the Director of Finance of a leading infrastructure company. I have been working with the company for 15 years. Nowadays I am feeling suffocated at work because the promoters are giving more importance to the newcomers than to the old employees. So, please advice.	24
5	I'm a very confident person. But, for the past few weeks I'm feeling a bit low because no one cares about my achievements. I have set up my own business and have taken it to a reasonable height. But now I feel like closing all this and going back to my hometown. Help me out.	28

CONTENTS

6	How can I develop a good customer base for my organisation?	32
7	Is it essential for the top management to be directly in touch with customers?	40
8	How to ensure a long term relationship with the customer?	44
9	The family business that I have taken over has not used technology so far. Is technology so important for business development in the new economy?	50
10	I am running a business house for the past 10 years. The rate of growth in the initial years were phenomenal. But for the last few years there is a marked plateau in my business. How do I improve it?	56
11	We have been, till now, focusing on high value products. We observe that there is a huge market for low value products. Should we diversify? We need clarity.	62

1

I am a self-made man and a first-generation entrepreneur. Though I am doing reasonably well in my business, of late, I am feeling a bit stagnated. Too many issues are demanding my personal focus. How do I take my business from here? Please help.

The fundamental understanding that is required is, "I may be better than all my people, but I cannot be at all places and I cannot do the job of all people." Organisations and people within the organisation can be developed only through delegation of accountable work. Delegation multiplies productivity; it helps fill a leader's day with accomplishments, instead of activities. Successful delegation is in finding the right balance between giving autonomy and holding responsibility.

The higher you are in the organisational ladder, the more responsible your position becomes as you are expected to demonstrate greater vision. Leadership is in decentralisation of work, but centralisation of responsibility. In delegation, the ultimate responsibility and control still remain with the delegator. On the other hand, the delegate has to be given sufficient autonomy to execute the task in their own way.

It is very important to give people the autonomy to express their own ways in executing a task delegated to them. People feel too discouraged and demotivated when managers thrust their way to do a task. Define the results and avoid defining the process. Nobody will work exactly the same way you do. Resist the temptation to intervene when a task is not being performed the way you want. Regular intervention will frustrate the delegate and deny them the chance to gain experience. Do not give advice, if the delegate can manage without it. Do not intrude too often and suffocate the delegate of their space. You need to give them the room to grow.

However, the foundation of successful delegation lies in the delegator's ability to brief the delegate clearly of the task to be performed. Work out a clear definition, which includes the objective of the task, the resources that are available, the landmarks and deadlines of the project, suggested procedures, skills required and the accountability factors. Discussing objectives and the final outcomes motivates your staff to embark on a task much more than treating them like school kids and discussing the processes involved.

In case you believe that your delegates do not have the core competency to proceed with the task, then training them in the competence required would be a more efficient and time-saving process, than to nag them on a daily basis with process and procedures. Good training builds people's capability and also motivates people to feel more valued as you have invested in their future.

Encourage the delegate to participate and create a checklist to ensure that nothing significant is omitted, that there are no overlaps and a proper schedule of the completion dates and final deadlines are listed. Let the checklist not only include the dos but also the don'ts. Incorporate a reporting plan. Ensure that the delegate and the delegator have a complete understanding of the checklist. This checklist will become the reference to review the progress of the task delegated.

Responsible freedom is always accountable freedom. Autonomy without accountability will create a reckless organisation. Accountability drives peak performance. Accountability ensures that the performer gets recognised and rewarded while the non-performer is identified and corrected. Accountability will help an organisation to avoid two of the most frequently repeated corporate blunders - rewarding or endlessly tolerating a non-performer and not giving a performer their due recognition. Lack of accountability will create an organisation where more than the performers, it is those who are able to project a performance who would get recognised. This will not only affect the goodwill within the organisation, but will also cause the loss of many capable human resources and will eventually crumble down the organisation.

People who stay the longest hours at work are not necessarily the most efficient... sometimes they cost the organisation more. People who stick to their schedules and do not turn up on holidays to work need not be insincere people... they could be the organised lot and a major asset to the organisation. So, create a system of accountability where performance can be monitored based on facts and figures, instead of opinions, 'what seems to be' and prejudices. What cannot be measured cannot be monitored. In what cannot be monitored, accountability cannot be established.

For people who consistently fall short of accountable standards, the mantra is simple. "Mend them. If not End them." Remember, one rotten tomato will spoil all other tomatoes. Cherish the seeds and throw away the weeds. People who consistently live up to the accountability standards of an organisation should be lifted and they will in turn lift the organisation. Remember, the person who follows the leader most efficiently is usually the person who develops into a leader most rapidly.

Though leadership is an art, like any art form, it can be scientifically learned and developed. ●

Leadership is in decentralisation of work, but centralisation of responsibility. In delegation, the ultimate responsibility and control still remain with the delegator. On the other hand, the delegate has to be given sufficient autonomy to execute the task in their own way.

2

How to develop a peaceful and happy environment at workplace?

Love, happiness, forgiveness, peace are all matured emotions. It is possible for individuals and communities to experience higher states of these beautiful emotions when they mature as consciousness. Let me explain what I mean by higher state.

Love is transactional if a receipt of a favour or disfavour is reciprocated; 'You did this for me so I will do this for you' type of love. A higher definition of love is to transcend that stage and be able to love with purity of intentions.

Everybody can be happy when everything is going good in their lives. That happiness you experience is the resultant effect of favourable events occurring at that point in your life. To experience happiness independent of what is happening in life requires a higher level of maturity.

To be peaceful in a perfect environment is possible by most. Even in a chaotic imperfect environment, to feel a sense of fulfilment and completeness is the higher state of peace. In those blissfully peaceful moments you feel that nothing has to be added or removed from you; you are enough unto yourself, complete unto yourself.

That kind of peace, permanently residing in you is the higher state of peace.

In spite of knowing that wrong has been done to you, by people whom you trusted and loved the most, if you still go ahead and execute this matured choice of being good to them, by forgiving them - that is living life out of a higher state of emotions.

'Love' in spite of, 'Happiness' in spite of, 'Peace' in spite of, 'Forgiveness' in spite of, are all very matured expressions of an evolved consciousness. The striving is to develop individuals and communities with these higher states of emotions. But at present our collective emotional maturity is far from this. Even the Buddhas, Christs, Prophets, Mahaveeras and Krishnas couldn't succeed in creating a peaceful world. Not everybody will be capable of those matured emotions all the time, especially in a work environment.

Well, what to do then?

We can create situations, in which people feel loved, peaceful and complete. We may not succeed in creating a life of 'Eternal Bliss' for our colleagues, but we can always create endless happy moments for them. In fact, creating happy moments is the best gift we can give to our team members. It is part of leadership to create avenues in which people are willing to let go of the past and move on into the future. Create a celebrative work environment in which people can come together in spite of their differences.

Creating a system by which we applaud the success of a team in public, somebody within the team gets recognised for a positive quality by the rest of the team on a weekly basis, celebrating birthdays and other festivals in the office environment, etc. can be done to make colleagues in an office feel very special. These initiatives can create work environments in which temporarily one finds that love, that happiness, that completeness, that let go and forgiveness.

So, to develop peaceful and happy office, resolve to create at least one happy moment for at least one colleague, every day of your work life. Walk into the office with a sense of purpose to create a happy moment for someone today and every day. I know it is difficult to keep people happy, but it's very easy to make people happy. Momentary happiness and moments of happiness are the easiest gifts we can give our team. So, let's make a commitment to endeavour to create happy moments for people. 'I will get everything I want from life when I help enough other people get what they want from life' being one of the laws of life... by creating happy moments for others, your happiness becomes a natural by-product.

How about a team picnic? How about giving a surprise gift when there is no occasion that demands it? How about at least one handwritten letter a week to different people, expressing your love and gratitude for the role they've played in making you what you are? How about a 'just like that' phone call to a colleague to let him know why you cherish your relationship with him? How about a sudden home visit to surprise someone on his birthday, as a gesture of love? How about packing a colleague's favourite food today? How about breaking the silence during an uneasy phase at office and easing things? How about volunteering to say a 'sorry' and unburdening the other of stress? How about losing once, just to make a victimised team member feel victorious? How about a non-official chit-chat at the coffee shop? The list is endless... only sealed by your creativity.

You cannot motivate another to remain in that state forever. But through your leadership, you can create environments in which people can be motivated to feel these positive states of emotions often.

It is leadership responsibility to make this happen systematically in regular periodicity with a surprise element built in it. Like how we refresh our computer screens periodically, we need to refresh the work environment too so that these buried beautiful emotions of teamwork, celebration, let go and feeling motivated can keep resurfacing in an organization.

Wishing you a peaceful work environment, which will certainly increase the productivity and profit. ●

With such high attrition rates how do we build a stable organisation?

The greatest issue most developing and growing organisations are facing is one of finding the right workforce and more importantly, the inability to retain the right workforce. What can be done about this? First and foremost, we need to recruit people more for their attitudes than qualification. More than knowledge and skill, assess the attitude of a person during the interview. By no means am I undermining knowledge, skill or qualification. It certainly gives the professional an edge.

There are four different aspects a person looks for and should be satisfied with, for them to feel attached to their place of work.

The first aspect is something all of us are familiar with - compensation. The challenge for most upcoming organisations is that they are looking for people, who are cheap and best, but in reality people are either cheap or best - they can't be both. Good people come at a good cost. How to resolve it? Let us denote the compensation of the employee as 'x' and the productivity expected of him as n(x). The current scenario is that you cannot do much about the 'x', for it is controlled by the market. Good employees are needed everywhere and at any price. However, improving the value of 'n' in n(x) is completely in your control, and that's what efficient management is all about.

The second aspect people need is that they should learn something new right through their tenure in the organisation. It isn't just enough for the purse alone to expand; the mind should also expand. It could be expansion of knowledge, development of new skill sets, refinement of attitudes or just some new information for information's sake - but people do not stay with organisations where their learning curve has stopped. So 'on the job' and 'beyond the job' create enough avenues for learning.

Thirdly, they need to ensure that their professional skills are developing during their association with the organisation. When a task that used to be done is now getting done in less and less time with greater and greater ease, then you know the professional within you is growing. Proper systems, the latest technology, effective leadership, clarity of tasks and responsibilities, and better and proven methods to do the same - when there is development in all these spheres, the individual finds the professional within, emerging. This is a key aspect that people look for in the organisation they work with.

Most of all, the employee has to see an organisational structure - a ladder of growth within the organisation that they can go up, if they serve the organisation long enough. This is the greatest challenge for all upcoming organisations. The founder of the organisation at the top and immediately below that, the rest of them, or as in some cases, a three-layered organisational structure - founder, manager and the rest - that's all we have. So most of them find that they can become the manager in a year, but several years later they will still remain a manager. This causes more manpower turnaround than any other single factor in most small and medium enterprises. Organisations that could resolve this particular crisis have become legendary organisations, and those which could not, have remained small and medium enterprises.

Organisational development is a huge and demanding mental game. What is possible for the Tatas and Birlas is possible for all of us. What one individual can do, everyone can do - just that we have to get the game right.

'On the job'
and
'beyond the job'
create enough avenues
for learning.

mahātria

4

I am the Director of Finance of a leading infrastructure company. I have been working with the company for 15 years. Nowadays I am feeling suffocated at work because the promoters are giving more importance to the newcomers than to the old employees. So, please advice.

First-and-foremost, if you have been with the company for 15 years and have ascended to the role of Director of Finance, you should feel a personal sense of responsibility when you see something is not going right in the organisation. The primary focus should not be on 'what is happening' but on 'what can be done'. After all, it is this organisation that has played a role in everything that has happened in your life in the last 15 years. You owe every morsel of food in these 15 years to this very organisation.

Fixing the blame needs no great intelligence. Causing a solution needs intelligence. In the long run, taking the most loyal employees for granted would not do any good to any organisation. So, as a first step, have a tête-à-tête with the promoters. Communicate long enough, communicate honestly and communicate without any personal agenda. Help them to reflect upon what's happening. A clerk can talk against the organisation. A Director of Finance should talk for the organisation. Live up to your chair. Just because the promoters are not living up to the chair, you don't have to fail to live up to your chair.

You may make a difference by opening the minds of the promoters. You may not make a difference. But, that's secondary. Now you will never feel guilty of not having done what you could have done. If it doesn't make a difference, of course, it is time for you to make a big decision.

It is always better to be in a better job than just a better paying job. Most of our waking hours are at work. So, a man who is feeling suffocated at work can never experience any fulfilment in life. If you decide to leave, then leave gracefully. If it must end, end gracefully. Don't keep bitching about the organisation and the promoters.

Simply put, in trying to degrade the promoters, don't end up degrading yourself. The options are simple. Either happily get along. Or happily get away. Never execute an option that's miserable to you or the other. So often, we either miserably get along or miserably get away. That's insane.

So, first show responsibility towards the organisation that made you. If you are not able to do much with the promoters, then show responsibility towards your own self. ●

Fixing the blame
needs no great intelligence.
Causing a solution
needs intelligence.

5

I'm a very confident person. But, for the past few weeks I'm feeling a bit low because no one cares about my achievements. I have set up my own business and have taken it to a reasonable height. But now I feel like closing all this and going back to my hometown. Help me out.

All of us feel drawn towards our roots. Your feeling a pull towards your hometown is quite natural. Whether it is an established business or permanent residency or citizenship or green card - however secure and settled you may feel in a new soil, something about you blossoms only with the thoughts of your hometown. However beautiful your city of progress is, and how much ever backward your hometown is, still what you feel in your hometown is intensely private.

Beyond the initial stages, money by itself is a poor motivator. But if you have a strong-enough reason as to what you wish to do with your financial surplus, then you will never lose your motivation for economic progress. If you build something with your money, then seeing it grow will certainly give you a sense of achievement. Then you will not need anybody to acknowledge your growth. Lift yourself wherever you smell success and in turn lift those in your hometown. ●

If you build something with your money, then seeing it grow will certainly give you a sense of achievement. Then you will not need anybody to acknowledge your growth.

mahātria

6

How can I develop a good customer base for my organisation?

The goal of an organisation should be to develop a buyer into an account, stage by stage. Today's customer is pampered with choices and over pampered with service. You can no more ask today's customer - "Do you want lower price, better service or high quality products?" No marks for guessing, for his answer will be - "All the three."

Today's organisations have to deal with a new breed of customers who carry a new customer ego - "I want to buy the way I want to buy." Most organisations are yet to catch up with this new breed of customers. As a result, customers feel over promised and under-delivered. Little wonder that the level of customer loyalty is low.

Loyalty implies that the customer buys from you repeatedly. A customer is one for whom buying from you has become a habit. Without a strong track record of repeat purchases, they cannot be termed as customers; they are only buyers. A buyer graduates into a customer when they make regular purchases. A customer develops into an account when they start purchasing across products and service lines, recommends to others to buy from you and most importantly, when they have become immune to the pull from the competition. An account is built over time. Organisational focus should be on building stable accounts rather than making a single sale. You transact with buyers, relate with customers and partner with your accounts. Increased customer loyalty will result in enormous cost saving in an organisation. It will mean reduced marketing costs, for customer acquisition costs a lot more money than getting an existing customer to make repeat purchases. It costs seven times more to generate a new customer than to get an existing one to repeatedly purchase from you. Customer loyalty also means reduced customer turnover expenses and increased cross-selling income.

As much as customer retention and account building have a positive impact on profitability, customer defection and losing of an account to competition has a negative impact. When you lose an account - a long term customer, it really affects your bottom line because a long-term customer does not tend to be overly sensitive to price.

The crucial benefits of building an account are: Sales go up because the customer is buying more from you. You also strengthen your position in the market when customers buy from you instead of your competitor. More importantly, marketing costs go down because you don't have to spend money on attracting a repeat customer, since you already have them. In addition, being a satisfied customer, they tell their friends, thereby reducing your advertising budget a little.

You are better insulated from price wars because a loyal customer is less likely to be lured away by a little discount. Finally, a happy customer is likely to sample your other product lines, thus helping you to achieve a larger customer share. This results in a scenario where the company spends less on acquiring new customers; consequently, it can afford to pay its employees better. Better pay prompts a chain reaction with a host of benefits. If a company is able to retain good employees, loyalty both within and outside the company improves - from employees as well as customers.

An account is built in stages. Stage one - a suspect. We call them suspects because we suspect that they may buy from us, but we don't know for sure. A suspect is one who has just become aware of your product.

Stage two - a prospect. A prospect is someone who must qualify on at least two key criteria: The need for your product or service and their ability to make the decision to buy. However, we disqualify a prospect at this stage when we know that they don't have the decision making ability to make the purchase, though they may have the need for the product or service. The sooner you disqualify a prospect, the better it is. Following up with an unqualified suspect or prospect is a waste of money, time and effort. The goal is to turn qualified prospects into first-time customers, then into repeat customers and eventually develop them into an account.

Stage three in building an account is transacting with first-time buyers. They make the initial investment on your product or service. A buyer will buy from you, and will also buy from your competitor. They are still making their post-purchase evaluation. From an organisational perspective, making a sale isn't the objective of the marketing process. It is the beginning of a lifetime relationship with the customer. It's a rare case when a customer can be sold something only once.

The first-time buyer is essentially trying out your product or service. If a continuing relationship has to be developed, it has to begin with the first purchase. If the first purchase does not satisfy the buyer, there will probably not be a second. They form a set of perceptions based on the buying experience. If the perceptions meet or exceed their expectations, there is a good likelihood that they will repurchase. This leads to stage four, where a buyer has turned into a customer. They repeatedly purchase from you.

Stage five is to develop this customer into an account. Every interaction should be seen as an opportunity to add value. It is important that your interaction with repeat customers works to deepen the relationship. These customers in turn respond with more information about themselves, becomes increasingly loyal and continues to push sales and profit upwards.

These actions enable the repeat customers to view your business not just as a building with a particular address or phone number, but as an organisation of human beings with whom they have formed a relationship. The relationship has progressed into trust; now you can be more proactive with the client. You have proved that you are dependable and accountable. You have now earned their confidence, and they increasingly seek your inputs on ideas and services. Value addition becomes mutual. They start encouraging others to buy from you. They talk about you and does marketing for you. When the customer goes out of the way to use your services, even if doing so means paying a little more, it shows that they have ceased to see you as a salesperson; they see you as an ally, a partner. When the relationship develops to this level, there is little a competitor can do to lure them away. You develop a strong and ongoing relationship that makes them immune to the pull from competition.

The goal within each stage of development is to take the relationship to the next stage of development. The goal of interacting with the prospect is to turn a prospect into a first-time buyer, the buyer into a customer and the customer into an account. Failure to develop a one-time buyer into an account robs the company of profit and valuable referrals.

A study shows that the probability of selling something to a prospect is only about 5% to 20%, while the probability of selling something to an existing customer is 60% to 70%. Surveys show that on an average, it takes about seven calls to close a first sale and only three to close a subsequent sale. So it makes business sense to develop accounts.

So instead of trying to think of a strategy that will appeal to the whole universe and coming up with nothing, concentrate on individual sales, individual customers, and groom them into accounts - this will lead to overall improvement in sales and profit.

How do I sell ten thousand tickets for the next game? Easy, you sell it one ticket at a time and then give them a good game! The future games will be taken care of. Take care of your customers' future and they will take care of yours.

Making a sale isn't the objective of the marketing process.

It is the beginning of a lifetime relationship with the customer.

7

Is it essential for the top management to be directly in touch with customers?

Your best customers are best prospects for your competitor. Insulate your best customers from competitor's attack; develop personal intimacy with your best customers. Rather than leaving to the moods, the whims and the fancies of individuals, develop systems which will ensure enough contexts to interact with people who are doing business with you. Here are a few simple contexts.

One third of all complaints come from customers who do not know how to use the product. So develop a system to interact with the customer and explain how to use the product and also motivate them to actually use the product. Even if the customer has bought your product, if they don't use the product, it doesn't improve their loyalty towards you. As important is selling the product and services to a customer, so important it is to get them to use the product and services. So, a follow up system is mandatory.

When you sell to a large organisation, several individuals may be involved in final decision to purchase. Once the initial decision to purchase is made, a fatal mistake is often committed. Sales and service personnel, and for that matter even the senior management, often end up dealing with day-to-day users in the customer organisation and not with the decision maker. When relationships are built with users and not decision makers, you will not be able to influence future buying decisions and will not succeed in empowering repeat purchases. Nurture and protect communication with decision makers.

Follow this simple system. Make 5 calls per day, write 5 personal notes per week and meet 5 people every month.

Assuming you work 250 days in a year:

250 days x 5 calls per day is 1,250 contacts

50 weeks x 5 notes per week is 250 contacts

12 months x 5 meetings per month is 60 contacts

Total contacts is 1,560 per year.

You can reach 260 people six times a year, 390 people four times a year or 780 people twice a year.

Every single thing we do is centred on one overriding aim: to get people to come back and make repeat purchases. If you look after getting repeat business, profits will take care of itself. A loyal customer is a precious commodity. Take care... not just of you but also your customers. ●

Insulate your best customers from competitor's attack.

mahātria

8

How to ensure a long term relationship with the customer?

Customer intimacy is achieved through operational excellence. Operational excellence means giving customers reliable products at competitive prices, with minimum difficulty in purchasing. It means giving customers the best available products and backing it up with outstanding service. It means segmenting a market with precision and then customising the services to meet the demands of that niche market.

How much ever we proclaim that the customer is the king, the reality is quite contrary. Two independent surveys on why customers change their vendors have revealed the following:

<u>Survey A:</u>

- 14% changed because their complaints were not handled.
- 9% changed because they were lured by the competition.
- 9% changed owing to proximity to the new vendor.
- 68% changed because they felt neglected by the existing vendor.

<u>Survey B:</u>

- 15% changed because the competition offered better prices.

- 15% changed because of quality problems.
- 20% changed because they felt completely neglected by the existing vendor.
- 50% changed because they didn't like the relationship approach of the existing vendor.

You should also know that a third survey revealed that customers who felt that their complaints were resolved have a repurchase rate of 54% and customers who felt that their complaints were resolved quickly have a repurchase rate of 82%. Most consumer electronics companies and automobile companies have started conducting regular free service weeks only to address this potential repurchase rate of 82%. Something is wrong if you aren't receiving complaints from customers. Don't be fooled into thinking that there are no unhappy customers. For all you know, the customer has already changed over to the competition.

Here are a few ways of developing customer intimacy.

1. If you have offered your customers the best available products, and have a track record of outstanding service, then once in a way remind your customers (at least indirectly) about what you have done for them. Most customers suffer from short-term memory loss. So, it is okay to implicitly remind them of the value you have added to them.

2. Once in a way, bring your best customers to your workplace and give them an experience of your work culture. Share the vision of your organisation with your customers; it'll make a world of difference.

3. Maintain customer service statistics and sales growth graphs and show it to your customers. Let them know that they are dealing with an organisation that is constantly growing.

4. A prompt 'thank you note' makes a greater impression than a detailed letter of acknowledgement sent a fortnight later. Develop promptness in customer related correspondence and communication.

5. Customers don't buy products or services. They actually buy certain satisfactions. Satisfaction is all about the emotional side of doing business with you. So, develop an empathetic personality and relate to your customers with your humane side on the forefront, rather than as a businessman who is always counting the profits. Add that humane touch to all your deliverables.

Satisfied customers are your best salesmen. Develop customer intimacy and your customers will develop a market for you. Take care of your customers and they will take care of your business. The competition is already at the door. Beware. ●

Bring your best customers to your workplace and give them an experience of your work culture.

Share the vision of your organisation with your customers; it'll make a world of difference.

9

> *The family business that I have taken over has not used technology so far. Is technology so important for business development in the new economy?*

Technology has changed everything - it is no more a question of who learns the best, but the question of who learns the fastest.

Economics is supposedly the study of allocation of scarce resources. The very definition of economics stunts economic growth, for it creates a limiting belief. It makes you believe that there is a scarcity of resources. In reality, there is no scarcity. Let us examine.

Oil was considered a waste 100 years ago. Today's silicon chip was yesterday's sand - dirt. Just two decades ago, if you were told that there would soon be a computer inside every car, you would have laughed. Yet today, the computer sitting inside every automobile is not only helping to reduce the pollution, but has also doubled fuel efficiency.

The native hunter did not consider land to be a resource. He used to take food off the land and then migrate to another land where food was available. Land was not a resource till the human mind found a way to cultivate it. Between 1930 and 1990, humans have developed technology by which they were able to harvest the same output in 1/100th of the land compared to the people of the 30s. In essence, they have increased agricultural productivity by 100%. Let us look at it another way - it is equivalent to having increased land by 100%.

Technology has changed everything. Technology is making all the difference. Anything to which we can add value becomes a resource. And technology is beginning to add value in ways we couldn't have imagined. How much resource you have, is defined by how you use it. Now, technology is defining and redefining what a resource is and also how much resource we have.

A dishwasher has replaced three cleaners. A washing machine has made two dhobis redundant. Earlier a few hundred people were required to lay a concrete ceiling, and today one concrete mixture lorry is able to perform the same. Owing to technology, one Narayana Murthy is able to produce what would have earlier required a few thousand people. One Ambani is able to produce more than what a few hundred industries together can.

Due to application of technology, lesser number of people are producing greater amount of results. The whole focus now is on increasing an individual's productivity. Now every individual is given a standard and is held responsible for upholding that standard.

The new corporate demand is that you need to continuously add value to yourself. You need to keep improving yourself.

Unemployment is the luxury of a good economy. Every time people lose their job to a machine, the society does not become poorer but actually becomes richer. It is the individual who becomes poorer. And when the unemployed individuals develop themselves into a new resource, either by learning a new skill or by developing a new proficiency, the society expands. And this is the new economy. In this new economy, what was considered the minimum is constantly expanding.

Luxuries have become necessities. Size of housing, basic necessities, salaries - the minimum is expanding in everything. Technology is consistently lowering the cost of what we produce, but we are continuously enhancing our taste for what we want. Today, 90% of all that we spend is beyond food, clothing and shelter. This is the new economy - an economy redefined by technology.

Now the big question is, how equipped are you to compete in this new economy. There's a new challenge that organisations are facing, a challenge called technology gap.

Technology is a better way of doing something that you are already doing. Technology gap is the gap between the way you are doing things and a better way of doing things, which has already been developed but you haven't implemented in your organisation. Technology gap will leave you way behind your competitors, assuming they have bridged the technology gap.

Bridging the technology gap will take you way ahead of your competitors, assuming you will be the fastest in implementing the emerging technology.

Two basic changes are required:

1. The question no more is - 'Can I also do it?', but 'Can I do it even better?' It all starts with the belief that there is a better way of doing what I am already doing. That's why people are no more paid for experience, but for expertise.

2. Technology changes so fast that what used to change in 60 years now changes in 6 years. The speed with which you learn something will determine the speed of your success. You can no more read a book and implement it next month - it will be too late. Tonight, latest by tomorrow. The skill you learn will become

obsolete in 10 years. You need to learn a new skill. So, it is no more a question of who learns the best, but the question of who learns the fastest.

You can no more live with contentment and compete in a world that is living out of greed. Today there are more successful people than ever, but they are not the same people who were successful yesterday. This new breed of people comprises those who have implemented technology and found a more efficient way of utilising resources. Consistency with speed, continuous value addition, pace of learning and constantly bridging the technology gap - these are the mantras of the new economy. Are you game for it?

10

I am running a business house for the past 10 years. The rate of growth in the initial years were phenomenal. But for the last few years there is a marked plateau in my business. How do I improve it?

In most businesses, the captain of the business is doing the same work in the same style as they were doing it a decade ago. Little do they realise that if they keep doing the same things then they will keep getting the same results. In many of the family businesses, from the previous generation to the present and from the present to the next, this style of working gets transferred. I know of businesses where the third generation in continuity is doing the same style of work but insanely expecting new results. In spite of enormous potential and expertise, these businesses remain businesses and never evolve into an organisation. Is there a difference?

A person runs a business. Systems and people within those systems run an organisation. A business is managed while an organisation is led. In business that one person remains the strength and weakness of the business. If it is an organisation, the weaknesses in the systems can be eliminated, strength and efficiency could be added to the system and most importantly more and more competent people can be added into the organisation to work within the system. Businesses are constrained by the physical limitations of the person whereas systems have no such physical constraints. There is a limit to how much a person can stretch but the scope to expand systems is limitless.

The prime responsibility of every businessperson is to evolve their business into an organisation. Initially you might have to run for the sake of your business but you cannot keep running behind your business all your life, that is life squandered. At some stage your business should run with or without you. The prime responsibility of every business head and the department heads within every organisation is to create systems, which would make at least a part of you dispensable.

What are most religions? They are just well organised institutions, where the founder of these religions scripted a system of dos and don'ts for people to abide by and the people who succeeded them have been marshalling their followers on the guidelines of these systems. Religions which had a system to follow has survived time and has kept growing even centuries after its inception. The rest, which were depended on a person like the present day business houses, have gone sand unto sand, dust unto dust.

In the early stages of one's work life, success is defined by the ability to produce eight hours of productivity by working for eight hours. As you grow, you should be able to work for eight hours and produce eighty hours of productivity. That is, now you have evolved a system through which you are able to produce eight hours of productivity from ten different people. Then it has to evolve to eight hundred hours and from then on to eight thousand hours of productivity and so on... This in essence is the growth of a leader from being a manager and this in essence is developing an organisation from being just a business.

The fundamental key to building an organisation is a shift that is needed in the attitude of the head of any organisation. People are too sentimental about their organisation and their position. They do not want anybody to take their position and in the process they cannot leave it either. This becomes their trap.

If you are too concerned about other people stepping into the ladder of your success then you have to remain in the same rung of the ladder to stop others from coming up. This may not affect others for they would get fed up and go in search of other ladders. It is you who will remain stagnant at the same rung of the ladder. On the contrary, if only you will let people step in and come up in the ladder of your success, as they raise themselves you will automatically go up another rung in the ladder. In fact, not only you will pull them up but they too will push you up.

The law of life is very simple. Anything you wish to transcend in life you must be willing to lose it.

Let us be very clear that the ultimate objective of building any organisation is to ensure maximum growth for maximum people in maximum possible ways. Do not get too attached to your methodology of working and lose sight of your vision. Please do not be a bottleneck to your own vision. Everybody cannot have a vision with a sense of grandeur, which you have.

There are enough people who can work and let them work through your system towards your vision.

Are you ready to make a part of yourself in your work dispensable? Are you willing to bring more hands, more legs and more intelligence to work on your objectives? Are you willing to design systems and make yourself too accountable to it? Are you ready for expansion? Are you willing to move from being a manager to being a leader? Are you willing to evolve your business into an organised organisation?

The epitaph of Andrew Carnegie who had millionaires working for him a hundred years ago reads: "Here lies a man who knew how to enlist in his service better men than himself." This is the art of leadership at its best. What shall your epitaph be? ●

Businesses are constrained by the physical limitations of the person, whereas systems have no such physical constraints. There is a limit to how much a person can stretch but the scope to expand systems is limitless.

11

We have been, till now, focusing on high value products. We observe that there is a huge market for low value products. Should we diversify? We need clarity.

For brand building, market positioning is very important. Consider these two laws of branding. 1. There is a market at every position. 2. However, a brand cannot hold two different positions in the mind of the market. In trying to do so, you will lose out on both.

Both Maruti and Hyundai are still struggling to gain market share of any significance in the premium car segment because of the brand position that they have built all these years as a 'Value for money' automobiles. However, in the position in which they have built, they enjoy phenomenal market share. Similarly, Mercedes and BMW are in the premium car segment and not in the 'Value for money' segment.

So, you have to make-up your mind on what position you want to operate, but you cannot take a dual position. If you do, you will lose out on both the positions. Alternatively, float a separate company, build an alternate brand and take the market in the other position. ●

***There is a market
at every position.***

***However, a brand cannot hold
two different positions
in the mind of the market.***

***In trying to do so,
you will lose out on both.***